FIREBIRD

ARROWSMITH
PRESS

Firebird

Kythe Heller

© 2023 Arrowsmith

All Rights Reserved

Second Printing

ISBN: 978-1-7346416-2-2

Boston – New York – San Francisco – Baghdad
San Juan – Kyiv – Istanbul – Santiago, Chile
Beijing – Paris – London – Cairo – Madrid
Milan – Melbourne – Jerusalem – Darfur

11 Chestnut St.
Medford, MA 02155

arrowsmithpress@gmail.com
www.arrowsmithpress.com

The thirty-first Arrowsmith book was designed & typeset by Farida Amar
for Askold Melnyczuk & Alex Johnson using Kinta & Lora typefaces.

Cover art by Marizó Siller, originally published in *Forecast Journal*.

FIREBIRD

kythe heller

7/17/23
for Malika,
with enormous love!
salám + meechum anbr

kythe Maryan
Heller

Why did you claim my heart
Before I'd given it myself?
Before it was mine to give.
And when, in this undoing, I could neither
Claim it nor give it,
When who I thought I was
Blazed and faded
In defective rhythm
And mind was stripped of knowing
And fled in terror from encompassing strangeness,
Why, when in my madness,
When mind betrayed heart,
And my heart belonged to You, not I,
Did You, in your arrogance or wisdom,
Return this heart to a shattered place
And replace her with another?

Now I have made claim
Of my self, my heart, my voice.
They are worthless to me.

ANONYMOUS SUFI

THE BURNING GIRL

I stood at the door of my life

but she was already there.

Her skin swollen.

And in her eyes

pain like a flower opening its body forever.

It was not she anymore

but the place marked out for the fire.

And at the center of the fire—her heart—

Life I thought I couldn't survive.

I had traveled so far to be here.

But how could I open the door and enter

my life

while she stood there burning?

There was wind somewhere

blowing in the trees. She

had locked herself out

for years

forgiving no one

If I look away from you for one second

I will lose you forever

I will lose the secret that you know

The burning girl's voice was singing. She had been waiting for me, she sang: I saw her squatting on the low roof outside my window. I shouted at her; she wouldn't come down. She was up there for hours, the snow falling—

Finally, late that night, she came down from the roof. She wouldn't look at me. She said it had been BEAUTIFUL up there—the aesthetics of it, blood against snow… Soon, she had a breakdown. When she was released from the hospital she was SORRY… For years she dreamed the snow had burned a hole in the back of her throat—: when she tried to speak, only cold air came through, wind—

We watched its movements at the edges of our skin, our faces impassive. And she asked nothing of me as she disappeared into whatever makes longing, and offered me her warmth and coldly marked me, as if fire and snow were joined together inside us, limitless and inconsequential as ash.

Death set her on the earth again
guilty of many crimes.

In a previous life, her name
Letitia, Latin for happiness

she perceived as an insane, spiteful joke.
Life itself should have been enough

but she wanted more. She wanted meaning.
And her given name sounded fake, like a porn star.

Perhaps that is why she was punished
with obvious zeal: she was not clever enough

to understand a lesson more subtle.
But that life is over.

She set fire to the paper bird.
She swung the flaming effigy through the sky
until it was gone.

Speak, said Death.
But I am a child.

Do not say you are a child;
you are no one you have ever been.

One time, she heard her father flipping the pages of the Wall St. Journal as she came to on the kitchen floor; he'd slammed her head on the edge of the banister when he threw her down the stairs. She could smell the leftover lobster in the air as she tested her body then limped past him, polite with rage—

She saw his face for a moment; he had started, she couldn't believe it, to cry … He was a little shaky and said he just wanted her to love him—

She walked out the front door barefoot into the snow.

And now the other side of the fire speaks to me. And I no longer know what page has been torn away between us, or what she has written in the ashes between my right shoulder and my left.

And there were so many things that would look—nice—if they were seen through flames ... The pile of trash outside the squat where she was staying looked so—inviting—she kept circling the block saying to herself: you're going to leave that alone, you're going to leave that alone ... She had to steel her mind not to think about setting—ah, everything!—on fire ... all of nothing or nothing of the All ...

In the classroom, it was beautiful but scary how the flame grew up so fast, devouring the flag and then the pasteboard wall, it was hungry—You could even begin to see everything that was already there clearly through the flame, everything outside of her matched her inmost intuition of reality ... as if there were no distance between the thought and its accomplishment, because thinking something made it be:

> everything is burning,
> has been and is always burning

What is the sheer fire that pools in the dark body before dawn? Fire no longer fire, so ancient, freed from the burning body that carries it.

The fire was famished: she fed it the lies and they suddenly seemed small. She held my thumb up to the flame; saw the fire, the plaster wall, my classmates and teachers, the politicians, my father–, everything that is–no bigger than my thumb.

I laughed and laughed. And the insane I thought: How can the fire hurt me when I too am made of fire? The fire's fingers, my fingers; the fire's eyes, mouth, tongue–, mine. Fire you are mine, you have always been mine: LIFE! LIFE! LIFE! LIFE! LIFE! And thought: I have a pure heart. I have annihilated everything that is created. I HAVE SEEN how it is so small, smaller than even my thumb, so small it is nothing. And I thought: it is nothing that is burning.

There was wind somewhere

blowing in the trees. We

brushed the twigs from our shadows and left

then returned to them empty.

I dreamed I was fire, she said

a ragged bandage over the light.

Then the bandage was torn away.

When I woke, I felt tears burning my skin—

has that no reality?

Why are you crying? Why am I?—

I didn't know who or what I was, only that I was

each syllable surrounded by a moving mouth of flame.

The twigs were so brittle, so small;

they drifted to the forest floor

then disappeared on the ground at our feet.

MATTRESS UNDER
THE OVERPASS

She could douse it with a gallon of lighter fluid. Light the match.
If she could watch like this always. Always to watch, never to
enter, never to feel the brightness catch and the fabric searing—
look, how the mattress holds everything the body refuses to
keep inside—leak, stain, spot, and mark—but nothing belongs

to it.

How will she hold herself if she cannot hold this? The
exhausting wheel of wounding and healing
burns.
                    Look inside the mattress, the suffering
burns. The desire
to heal again through suffering burns. I don't want to feel, but
how could I bear not feeling—

She's been floating for years, hovering somewhere above her body, I said. Is this the bed she must enter, is this where she was conceived, in a bed of fire? Wings lifting up mouth open calling over the gauze of smoke, the dim orange hum coming and going over them.

Did she know what knowing is, as the bed burned from the outside in, black flakes oranging at the edges, then breaking off in pieces to spark out on the sand? Which was the blaze that burned through the outer husk of her? Which seared into the mattress, into every fiber of tissue and flesh

to burn away what she was, what she meant to become—

There where the wound is open, utterly still in its need, so completely still in hunger as the sway of yellows swell and fall over it, swell and fall–

The skin of eyelids covering the whole of a body, eyelids all flickering, ready to exist, along the whole horizon of its being, ready to exist, a unified weeping like the emergence of the soul, what do the dead want from us, what is the light of the inside, light meeting light like mirror meeting fire–

The body of eyes everywhere a joyful sobbing: everywhere a crackling wash of cries where the glowing coals emerge

just at the center of the fluff of ash and blackened fabric–

Last night I felt the flames climb in at last to the inner core; they found the wire mesh of the mattress twisted in its skeleton of light, its body of glowing gold in the black. Joy or anguish, to be born in fire, in the elemental moment, to feel the flames coursing over my bones, caressing every cell with light

until at last the fire bent down low over
the rib cage,
and reaching, reached in.

My shattered chest was coiled like wire.

Heart melted down to a single pour.

X

"Then that heart ... melted into the form of liquid pearl, which wobbled, flowed over, and rolled, drop by drop, to shatter into resplendences of grace ... scattered as seeds of life and as light rays ..."

THE SPIRIT NEITHER SORTS
NOR SEPARATES

Q: You know the photographs of the dead in heaps,
tangled in each other's arms?

A: Even when I was whole all I wanted was to be healed.

We separated the X-rays into piles: keep and throw away.

You made minimum wage and I made a dollar more

wheeling Benny to the bathroom.

Frozen and locked in his chair

he pressed an automated screen with his tongue;

he would type SHIT and FUCK to make us laugh.

At times, our skeletons would resplend.

We stroked their wounds

reached our fingers into their light shadows.

Believed in their x-ray dream.

Our fingers caressed the bones of all these broken strangers.

There are things death touches that we do not know.

There are things death touches with the intimacy of a girl

kneeling in a field of wind alone.

Once I lay awake to watch my lover's face as he slept.

His forehead! His cheek! His lips!

Any situation can be an empty form, I continued.

Like ours, you said. A secret conduit for the language of light.

We brushed the bones from our shadows and left

then returned to them empty, reading the X-rays like tarot.

It hurts to remember you.

Your head bowing below your heart.

Your eyes like two cups full of blood.

We were "developmentally disabled."

Then the Goddess of Love spilled a thousand seeds on the floor

and commanded her to separate them into piles.

Earth has painted me white

and adorned me with feathers.

Given me this mask of fire

fashioned from the skin of my inner thighs.

When I am laid on the altar

and my life shatters, Earth says:

The existence of the world depends on

the heart's ascending flight.

(something sobbing in me all the time, all the time)

When my lover touches me, what I feel in my body

is like the awkward thrashing of a bird

slipping out from two palms, as the breath catches—

each moment the limit of the flame

to which it owes its flying.

I do not know if it's called pleasure or pain.

I feel him directly.

When he left, I said

Psyche threw his clothes into the street

stood in the kitchen weeping

unable to wash the spoon his lips had touched.

I told other lies while we worked,

and took Benny to the bathroom.

The beauty of your fingers blessing the strangers' bones

soared up through me

with a loneliness like being in love.

No one will remember you

if I don't write this. You are probably dead by now

with your degenerative disease.

We were shivering in the faulty florescence.

When she forgot to eat, I said, her friend

stuck pieces of tape on her shoes that said EAT.

Inside me a girl is making

a cairn of dead birds: for a moment

her hand is held out and steadied, as if to touch

a rain too fine to feel.

I thought I found you in passionate grief.

I thought I discovered you at last

in radiant loss.

I thought you wanted me so broken I could not separate

broken from whole.

In the leaping laughter and in the inconsolable.

See inside the laughter and climb into the seed, you said.

See the X-ray light

flowing over your bones.

Say the word that will release me. Let me begin again.

I am far. I am so far.

I am stupid. I surrender everything.

A cartload of X-ray negatives. Empty.

Contains the language of the underworld, and more.

I cannot even call you by your name in the dark

you have no name you are

this close you are nothing, and closer.

RUNAWAY

There were things that happened with fire. Before, when I could not speak. I am not certain that fire is the correct word. The first was the burning inside the girl, then completely separate from her. On its own. The second was a flock of skeletons, flaming birds. She was frightened. There were fire marshals signaling. This is illegal, they said. With enormous effort, I prevented myself thinking the thing inside the match that wanted out. And then, because I had to, because the fire could not be prevented, I wrote this.

Liquid gases, messy curls and swollen skin, the burning girl flushed transparent against the rough brown of the couch. She offered us warmth and light, but we were frightened of her fatal blood disease, of her beatific face and rapes. We were frightened of her, despite her bookbag and stuffed octopus. When she left, it was November, the first snow before winter. What we did was, write her into the Client Book, under Open Cases.

And now, peer into the book again: isn't it your face there in the mirror? Step in, she said; read the language of light backwards, through my oracle bones.

Behind the runaway shelter were the other houses, intensely nondescript in the pale grey sky.

Behind the girl was the fire.

At the edge of the fire was a seam, blackened needles sewing a spectral garment she remembered and forgot. A dense membrane of blood reached the surface of her skin. The threat of underneaths completely separate from her, moving together in a flushed permeability. The flame that ventured outside the mind. I stood there not knowing what to do. Where had she gone, I thought, watching her bare footprints in the snow.

Later, her eyes were still, intensely peaceful against her fevered skin as she opened them. Above her, the fire was thick with long branches that reached impassably with colors I could not identify. In the seconds before the surgeons came in to operate, she reached up, her arms criss-crossing frantically, marking an X beneath the stainless steel.

When I remembered the scene later, in New York, the image of a cairn of dead birds superimposed itself on her chest. Her upper body thick as a tree trunk. I thought her heart must be a nest—the body a shelter for curved space, the site of the pyre. Instead of arms, she had streaks of light.

The lightning sky like scars on a face. Leftover stars fleck the upturned cheek above the houses.

In the mirror, all the sparks stir. A mirror is a liquid fever.

How the skin shrivels, where her feet are too cold, making prints in new snow. She remembers everything that has yet to happen. As one does, reading a mythological tale. She left. She was a runaway. Her feet were heavy. Her feet were touching the snow. Her feet were reaching and reaching: going out to the edges, where the color is.

Street signs rising in rows, automatically. Because it's November, we can't see the bare arms or tufts of snow melting in the V of the tree trunk. Now the leaves want to be fire. But the fire waits. One can almost see a flicker in the face of the man who laughs with me, crossing the street on my bike and almost hit by a car. One can almost see it in our shared eyes. But deeper in. Leaves imagining themselves ablaze. Then ablaze.

He—the Turkish man—lifts some luminous words from the café table, holds them out with the invisible edge of a blade, holds them up to show me. When I reach out my fingers to touch more of their skin, he stops my hand with his. When I ask, when was the last time you cried, he says that he studied acting for two years in LA where he was taught never to inhabit a role completely. If you have to cry for real, he says, you should go into the rehearsal room where you can be alone.

Even so, we part at 3pm with plans for a backdrop, a theatrical forest where a fire line has been blazoned with a cross, our shuffling feet smearing its chalk. He says: "an incineration celebrates, perhaps, as Derrida writes, 'the nothing of the all' … Ah no, above all not Phoenix (which for me, moreover, is first of all, in my fundamental language, the mark …"

The burning forest behind or in front of us. Culture like a walk-on character in our movie. I want to say something more, but the class is waiting for me to make a presentation on the Simurgh. I didn't know what his name would sound like.

I want to eat everything but I can't do that here. They would know what I am by the look in my eyes. My intolerable heat. At the edge of the forest no one knew I was there, not the others or my invisible mother with her coat of many colors.

In my movie, I run toward her as she waits for me on the mark of ochre chalk. She opens her coat like two wings and I rush in.

To her cloth heart, her cleft of holy fire.

In the newspaper, she—the runaway who is 32 but thinks she is 16—demands a blood test to prove that she is not related to her father or mother. That this can happen: one of the selves runs away from the other ones. There are so many flames, you would think we could spare this one or that one. Crystal Bullitt. Others, alone with the alone, survey the place marked out for the fire. Never growing older than when it happened. Never wake up from the dream. A clue. A reporter's account. I look for the burning girl and I find other runaways who have never come home.

"You should set this in history more, make a strong statement about abuse. Neglect. A socio-political critique of the shelter system. With more details of the trauma." What is the sheer light that pools in the dark body before dawn? Light no longer light, so ancient, freed from the body of air that carries it?

The girl. You cannot even remember her name. Ash. Eye-bone. Cinder of skull. The residue mute. I did not see her grave. I did not see how she could be properly buried in a town that was all one blade, balanced on the knife at the table's edge. In your town, or in the place where you were a child, was there an abandoned shed? Was there a river beyond, the smell of wet earth? Imagine a dense, leafy undergrowth, a musty shed filled with equipment, soil planters, buckets, everything dusty with age. The edge of the forest: abandoned shed where the leaves overhang the ordinary blue of sky. It has grey leaves at night and blackened grass. But I don't know if it was day or night. I knew I might be guilty of her death and I waited, my heart beating rapidly. I looked at the planting urn but couldn't remember if. I might have killed her. I knew that somehow the river was rising, thought I must have. My guillotine eyes. My innocent talons.

The air was stale. With cold fingers I lifted the skin where she had been—bruise-marks, bleeding—where the fingers of others had torn strips from her many-colored coat. All crimson orange flames like skin from my previous life.

A feral girl is gritty, complex, thin. To beat her, you had to run her down on the street, drag her back by the hair. Extinguish her. One of many entries to the underworld. No. It's not enough to know what she knows. I want—what she is the metaphor for. What she is—beyond metaphor.

How a runaway girl is like a fire: she slips out from the shelter, onto the street of Sleepfield, and runs, her shirt flickering out behind her. The method of fire is one of pure need accompanied by the husk of the body. The girl's desperation flames out from her to meet the city's tense mirror, producing, if one narrows the eyes, a threatening display.

I am writing for you, in November. It's cold. The fire girl was like a fetus, hidden, compelled to emerge. A match with fire inside like a seed. I remembered her in the room of the shelter lit by small pink lamps. I illuminated them in my mind—No. How could I visualize retrieval when it's the facts themselves that need to be explained? Chronologies of escape record only the perimeter, the edge of the forest, not the transformation. What gives light must suffer burning, escape what ravishes. Castigates.

It does not work to follow. Of course it does not. But it's better than shapeless trash or nothing at all. I must continue writing. It's so cold. A text is a mirror, the report of a crime.

I was almost to the forest. I was almost to the forest when he reached out and grabbed me back by my hair, my mouth forced open to an O.

What is the procedure of escape? Become invisible not to risk detection. Pretend everything is normal. I was a girl buying a train ticket, to visit someone in Boston. Perhaps an aunt. No one knew the thing inside me that wanted out.

Scritch. The body a piece of sandpaper on the edge of the matchbook. The escape. How one is trained to pretend. It's only a match. It will not feed. I will not satisfy its hunger. I promise to kill it as every insatiable thing must be killed in order to live. Wanting to be found. To burst into flame.

Rise and eat. Rise and eat. Devour.

She was calling to herself

As if across a vast distance–
But she could not answer; she had fled too far inside.

And because she could not answer, Everything answered:
as pain–

Oh pain was generous! First it gave her
a throat crowded with wings, thrashing black
shrieks and claws inside her skin.

Then it gave her

A garment of smoke

Leftover bones–

THAT HEART

Time Does Not Exist

Alone, the girl she was

became the *pieta*

in the basement of the museum,

every detail of drapery and gesture perfected

in the pour of her weeping mind.

Even the silence would turn her to stone;

whatever she encountered, she became.

As though already she knew

the beautiful dead man like a child

cradled in her marble arms. And felt the chiseled

grief waiting in the rough unfinished stone

too huge yet to enter her face.

Let Me Begin Again

Let me touch lightly with my hand all I have known.

Leave all that is mine on the street again.

Let strangers tune the guitar, hold the dress up to check the fit.

Let the nametag be torn from the suitcase. Thrown away.

Let me be no one again.

Let my bed be bare ground.

Bus station grass where the deer once lay.

Child fort in the park, indefensible and inviolate.

Let the baby's wage be my value.

The shelter my home. Time and place.

Let me pass through all I've left behind, until the goodbye enters.

Train me to darkness.

Let me know what it is to know.

Begin with: offering a leaf.

Every breath.

Joy streaming through our bodies

clenched together on the top floor.

Offer the grief. The squirrel's head crushed by a heel.

The silence inside the burnt-out tree.

Let me learn to sleep alone in the wind.

Take only the night sky, its endlessness.

Take the mattress under the overpass, the bed no one else wants.

Nothing you could not gather at the last hour, visible or invisible.

If it comes to that. It will always come to that.

A *Flor de Piel*

Inside me a girl is kneeling, but I do not know her.
Touching and not touching
the shroud of roses she sews petal by petal
on the floor.

As if what her fingers touch
could tell us what we have lost–
How everything will be lost.

I can hear her sharp keening
as roses disremember into a new shape.

As if what is absent speaks through us.
As if we remember everything that has yet to happen.
And the awkwardness of the shroud
arranging itself without the body.

As if only being dead were fragile enough
for what the earth has to say.

Inside me her eyes grow darker. Blackened needles
sewing a spectral garment she remembers and forgets.

My body gets smoky, she says. Gets holes in it.
A country I can no longer tolerate,
precarious as space and time,
two forms of motion as a cross. The body is

a metaphor, its desires
nails to be removed ...

The mark a needle makes as it appears
disappears between the folds.
Her body sutures the dark border
between the roof and the moon.

Things that enclose me and things I cannot touch.
They are so near.

Inside me a girl was kneeling. She returned home
after a long journey
but home was never there.

(Something sobbed in her all the time, all the time.)

The small flame in her shivered like an eye.

Did she climb in?
Part her shattered chest and
lick at the rose petal honey
flowing over her bones?

What did they have to do with her happiness, or grief.

She was that last, unspeakable thing:
the body like a field
stripped to bare ground, then burnt—

Only the soul kept searching the ground;
no one knows how to comfort it.

It's like the moment a stranger,
say, at dinner, asks you: where's home? and you hesitate—
then lie, and tell him you live in Brooklyn.

What you see in that moment is
what the soul sees:

Why should I lie? Is my voice
like the blackened earth, the voice of cinder?

Who do you think you are
soul skipping from lightworld
to lightworld

like a stone through its
smeared reflections—

A bird flew through my body!

Incapacitating joy?

The wound had happened before.
Joy—before
I knew it was mine—wheeled and
flew through me
before I knew I am not

Soaring the blackened field
a bandage inside my body
torn off from separateness—

Messenger
never knowing the difference
between your own heart pumping 1,640 beats a minute and
the heart of the world into which you fly.
What trust.

That must be why birdcalls are
beyond loneliness,
so intimate and wild they glide right into the depths of you
and disappear there—

so completely your own you hardly know what is
singing in you at all—

I have crawled straight through the mountain. Straight
through the
block of brightness that was
your body, Love—that bewilderment.

[...]

Now there is no amazing scent of musk
rising from your skin when I lift the bedclothes—
[...] for a moment, I hold the night sky to my chest
and all its fragility.

In that heart,
what point is there in dying or being born again?

Acknowledgments

Grateful thanks to the editors of *The American Poetry Review*, *Alaska Quarterly Review*, *The Harvard Divinity Bulletin*, *Periphery*, *WICK (Harvard University)*, *Slush Pile*, and *Bandit Press*, for their kind acceptance and publication of several of these poems in earlier versions.

I am especially grateful to professor Kimberley C. Patton (Harvard Divinity School) and the Harvard Art Museums for commissioning "A Flor de Piel" for the 2016-2017 exhibition and conference entitled "Topography of Loss: A Symposium on Doris Salcedo."

Immense gratitude to Askold Melnyczuk, Ezra Fox, Farida Amar, and everyone at Arrowsmith Press, for your selfless help as editors and supporters of these poems. I wish also to thank with love the Wild Geese, the Yogi Witches (Sahaj Kaur [Shelley Loheed], Hari Dass Kaur [Biliana Angelova], Dharam Singh, Beth Fincke, and Laura Dolp, Heather Cox, Ashley Clements, Alex Johnson, Ariana Reines, Christina Davis, and Vision Lab, for spaces of nourishment and creative light. Special thanks and love also belong to Myra Diaz, for your insightful reading of an earlier version of these poems.

Blessings of gratitude and love to Fanny Howe, whose reading of these poems was invaluable as the book came into existence.

The quote on page 16 is from *The Resonance of Allah* by M.R. Bawa Muhaiyaddeen, published by The Fellowship Press in Philadelphia, PA. *Firebird* is dedicated with everlasting gratitude to M.R. Bawa Muhaiyaddeen.

KYTHE HELLER is a poet, essayist, interdisciplinary artist, and scholar. She is author of the poetry collection *Firebird* (Arrowsmith), *The Soul Conveys Itself in Shadow / El alma se mueve en la sombra*, an edited collection of translations (Stenen Press, with Carolina Gómez-Montoya), *Thunder Perfect Mind*, a text and image artist book with photographer Meka Tome (Forecast), and several critical essays on mysticism and poetics, published by Cambridge University Press, Akron Series in Contemporary Poetics, and Harvard Divinity School Graduate Journal. Her writing has appeared in *The American Poetry Review*, *Tricycle*, and *The Southern Review*, among other publications; she is grateful for fellowships and grant awards from Harvard University, The Mellon Foundation, John D. and Catherine T. MacArthur Foundation (awarded to support a writing fellowship in poetry at The MacDowell Colony), Virginia Center for the Creative Arts, Vermont Studio Center, and The Community of Writers. Her multimedia film and performance work has been exhibited nationally and internationally. She is editor-in-chief of *Forecast Journal* and teaches on the faculty of the Language and Thinking Program at Bard College. Currently, she is completing a doctorate at Harvard University.

ARROWSMITH is named after the late William Arrowsmith, a renowned classics scholar, literary and film critic. General editor of thirty-three volumes of *The Greek Tragedy in New Translations*, he was also a brilliant translator of Eugenio Montale, Cesare Pavese, and others. Arrowsmith, who taught for years in Boston University's University Professors Program, championed not only the classics and the finest in contemporary literature, he was also passionate about the importance of recognizing the translator's role in bringing the original work to life in a new language.

Like the arrowsmith who turns his arrows straight and true,
a wise person makes his character straight and true.
                                  – Buddha

Books by

ARROWSMITH
PRESS

Girls by Oksana Zabuzhko
Bula Matari/Smasher of Rocks by Tom Sleigh
This Carrying Life by Maureen McLane
Cries of Animal Dying by Lawrence Ferlinghetti
Animals in Wartime by Matiop Wal
Divided Mind by George Scialabba
The Jinn by Amira El-Zein
Bergstein edited by Askold Melnyczuk
Arrow Breaking Apart by Jason Shinder
Beyond Alchemy by Daniel Berrigan
Conscience, Consequence: Reflections on
Father Daniel Berrigan edited by Askold Melnyczuk
Ric's Progress by Donald Hall
Return To The Sea by Etnairis Rivera
The Kingdom of His Will by Catherine Parnell
Eight Notes from the Blue Angel by Marjana Savka
Fifty-Two by Melissa Green
Music In–And On–The Air by Lloyd Schwartz
Magpiety by Melissa Green
Reality Hunger by William Pierce
Soundings: On The Poetry of Melissa Green edited by Sumita Chakraborty
The Corny Toys by Thomas Sayers Ellis
Black Ops by Martin Edmunds
Museum of Silence by Romeo Oriogun
City of Water by Mitch Manning
Passeggiate by Judith Baumel
Persephone Blues by Oksana Lutsyshyna
The Uncollected Delmore Schwartz edited by Ben Mazer
The Light Outside by George Kovach
The Blood of San Gennaro by Scott Harney edited by Megan Marshall
No Sign by Peter Balakian

CPSIA information can be obtained
at www.ICGtesting.com
Printed in the USA
BVHW040718060623
665442BV00001B/30